Here it is: a dope jam of dictions; a remixed, multicultural, polyphonic dance of vocabularies; a language of high stakes, hi-jinx, and hybridity. *TwERK* is subversive, vulnerable, and volatile. *TwERK* twists tongues. *TwERK* tweaks speech. Reading these amazing poems mostly makes me say, Wow! Open your ears to take this music in, open your mouth to say it out loud. And: Wow!

TERRANCE HAYES

If the genre Black-American cosmopolitanism exists, Diggs is at the helm. Putting a new twist on an Ezra Pound-like gaze, Diggs approaches Black-American Orientalism with a coy wit and jovial approach that does not absolve—yet joyfully disarms both author and reader. Above all *TwERK* is a delightful celebration, word-play born out from the rigor that finally speaks our language (even if we don't know it yet). I've been Twerked and contrary to my worst fears, my wife loves the results!

MIKE LADD

WARNING: After reading *TwERK*, you may experience vibrant, dancing colors like when you close your eyes and stare at the crazy shifting shapes behind your eyelids. LaTasha's brilliant poems vibrate me back to that unbridled youth of boundless madness, love and joy. *TwERK* testifies that LaTasha is not just a poet but an anthropological myth-making DJ whose words will have your imagination on the dance floor kicking it till your goosebumps start to sweat! This is a must-read for real for real! Oh, did I mention she speaks like 10 different languages?

CHARLES STONE III

TwERK

Second printing, 2014

ISBN: 978-0-9885399-0-7

Cover design by Douglas Kearney.
Interior design and typesetting by HR Hegnauer.

Belladonna* is a reading and publication series that promotes the work of women writers who are adventurous, experimental, politically involved, multiform, multi-cultural, multi-gendered, impossible to define, delicious to talk about, unpredictable, & dangerous with language. Belladonna* is supported with funds granted by the New York State Council on the Arts, the O Books Fund, and from generous donations from our supporters. The book is also supported with a grant from the Council of Literary Magazines and Presses and the Jerome Foundation.

Cataloging-in-publication data is available from the Library of Congress.

Distributed to the trade by
Small Press Distribution
1341 Seventh Street
Berkeley, CA 94710
www.SPDBooks.org

Also available directly through
Belladonna*
925 Bergen Street, Suite 405
Brooklyn, NY 11238
www.BelladonnaSeries.org

* deadly nightshade, a cardiac and respiratory stimulant, having purplish-red flowers and black berries.

TwERK

LaTasha N. Nevada Diggs

BELLADONNA* 2013

contents

And the earth was of one language,

and of one speech.

Genesis 11:1

anime

Black Boy, O Black Boy, is the port worth the cruise?
Melvin B. Tolson, "Alpha"

mista popo™ hollas @ jynx™

In 2004, Viz began to downsize Mr. Popo's large lips digitally

Mista Popo,   in the order of djinns to proceed —
from blue-black to purple to pink.
There was nothing less visible than this red tire poised to smile.

                    Lips disputed, disappearing, reappearing.

          Mista Popo adjusted his turban of starch white.
          Mista Popo was determined to prevent Kami from tappin Jynx's ass before him.

                    Mista Popo said: oh bodacious Zwarte Piet,
                              How does the butterfly garden thrive
                              for my big ole kettle belly?

An extra scoot never too robust for my flying carpet.

          So croon,
                    holla at me Jynx,   holla at me Jynx,

                    holla at me Jynx w/ some soba on the side.

          Let's fly away!

Mista Popo want that corn husky hair.

Mista Popo want that hibiscus round your neck.

Mount me with your mammy tie-dyed kimonos.

Go-go ganguro manga mamasita izza to my dizza...

Blessed be your bleached pastel purikura ketai.
So that we both know: your tan from Shibuya right?
Now is your booty valley Honey   or Janet Jackson?

Is you is that face of flattery and kuragari or is you is my dark exception?
Darky girl, where you get dat cup size? Ain't no Koreans up in here that buoyant.

Who's your Smoochum™ daddy?
Mista Popo want Pikachu™ heated.
Trust Son Goku™ can't land a punch.

Mista Popo can be your primitive ashtray.

That's right jubilee wind your hips,
shake it like a hoochie,

bounce it yamamba chibi,

dazzle your wog eyes;   wave them Mickey gloves.

My dragon ballz swing low for you propa:
you give Mista Popo nosebleeds.

dutty gal

        titanium, boom shocka, kill di woofa.
thrash reverberating neatly polish mih ride.
              hyphy dancehall — no can
    hear tings demur.
titanium, boom shocka, kill di woofer
whine mih curvature: cause a road slaughtah.
              ain't neck breaking like dutty
    when she whine.
        titanium, boom shocka, kill di woofa.
thrash reverberating neatly polish mih ride. sih?

pistology

kyooryoku na transmitter de cielo, *mighty transmitter of heaven,*

      blessed visor de imagen, *blessed viewfinder,*

           captured hoshano of hikari. *captured radiation of radiance.*

dotekina kinescope, *color kinescope,*
      globalizing sounds unit modulation.
                     O' fallacious shizukesa.
                       O' fallacious peace.

           fukyu no meisaku!
           fukyu no meisaku! fukyu
           no meisaku! *immortal masterpiece!*

anata wa absorb my peripherals, *you absorb my peripherals,*

      contrasting en medio real time y *contrasting between real time and*

           Buffy la matar de vampiro. *Buffy the vampire slayer.*

azucarado reflection of stale tecnologia.
      sweet reflection of stale technology.

suteru realism,
giver of realism,
my gabriel blow horn de propaganda.
my Gabriel blowhorn of propaganda.

fukyu no meisaku! fukyu no meisaku! fukyu no meisaku!
immortal masterpiece!

mediator of media,
      grocery bag stuffer of life's marketed indulgences.

yo reso para ti *I pray to you,*
      mi amplified padre, *my amplified father,*
      mi prime time okaasan. *my primetime mother.*

watakushi no/closed captioned espiritu santo…
my closed-captioned Holy Ghost…

by broadcast, you are my sagrada communion, you are my Antichrist.

bacche kā pōtRā

bloom, the dandelion dance of Keisha's mane. a Wave
of bush. her kitchen pearls & truffula treetops.
begin the traction. tug. creamy crack. lye ale. wave

so long. mares can be jumpy. but baby-girl's plumes burnt.
crunchy bacon. her puberty looms early. fizzled particles
stuck to a flat iron. diapers don't detect ovarian cysts. wave

adieu corkscrew. the follicles doomed. scorched sirens —
coils used to protect from ultraviolet. all for a ponytail? wave
to trichologist mama. to groom was spiritual once. now gray
pus from scalp drench tissue. lingering, a caustic perfume.

blind date

FADE IN:

INT. / EXT. Eddie Van Halen rock riff in background — DAY

       flat matte TMZ graph-o-matic reads: E.P.I.S.O.D.E. 3.18.02
       crop & bedazzle perpendicular to a fast fade

we see PAULA GARCIA (30s)
       sassy southern belle, open-minded pet photographer
       likes men who claim sincere.

we see MACK ATTACK (40s)
       divorced, fun lovin' wino, mid-life cruiser:
       "goes for girls with a butt."

                  HOST (V.O.)

       beefeater chatterbox guzzler,
       jacuzzi silicone,

                      honey bunny.
flash tony the tiger,   crackerjack preacher,   pop-up mama.

       is eric's down to earth attitude what carle is looking for?
       can *rrrrrricco* be *z* lover not *z* fighter elizabeth needs?

PAULA GARCIA

(CALM) washer board,   backside
                 speed bar, candy factory.
pom-pom wax, mud bath,   (SEDUCTIVELY) lap up a ham hock for a belly dance.
                 taxi ride,   escort.
                 eye doctor,

                             overboard.

MACK ATTACK

(EXCITEDLY) her bikini lini, maxi pad, plops spots on g-strings.
            jail house tattoo on my boo-boo, ain't waterproof.
            (LEANING IN CLOSER) waddle waddle id to ego to no goodbye kiss.
            poker shot pucker, no can diss the vagina
            and *please*, won't ya flash the juicy flat-liner:
            (O.S.) *once you go rican you never go seekin.*

END SCENE

Sunspot

flensing the bounce, the clap cheeks make, boys are
adored too easily. or perhaps the treasure trove we

deem invoked by twerk. love offering? booty without
arcane clues? rump could be scrolls the pirates desire
buried in the crease of flesh; or even thoroughbred mouthed
by knees that meet upon instruction and beat. Who

discovers the loot? cheap stilettos draw blood. are
we penors of lace fronts? our muskets black thighs? we

perspire into amphorae enough to erect and reward. in
15 cubits resides our platinum peek-a-boo chests. the
glare: a sunspot adorned just for a night of presence.

Benihana

she wishes Rocky usada *cookbooks*   rūma moe : *bedroom cuisine*

niho : *nitro* libido *samurai diced & sliced*

sweet & sour calypso in a hotei tiki mug   baby-girl knows he burned the rice

she wishes Rocky a rave kei : *at* Che Fong's bungalow

uru : *enter* the binghi harps played by Duke Lukela

she wishes Rocky tossed oriental shrimp y huevos in a hot tub

korā : *over there* Kono Kalakaua is manning the grill

his backgammon trophy awaits him in heaven

an afterlife supply of jheri curl kits

saketini on the house   a rave in his name

in virtuous timbre she mantras, "*come now, no more faking blackouts.*"

Japanese custom   Rocky's poly

konā: there, ka tākaro ngā tamariki ki waho with Ginsu knives

the children will play outside

Chin Ho Kelley is attending to them

she wishes Rocky muziek di zumbi, a day with Sizzla in a hot air balloon

a Hummer converted ice cream truck

te tae : *the color of* kikorangi : *blue*

a collage of sugar cones & strawberry road on DVD

his wrestling pecs in high-res   he did not patent the fortune cookie, but…

pequino manu, no strife from Bobos down Lenox Ave.

pūrnimā : *night of full moon*, night of vaudevillian lineage
someone did not read the omikuji

she wishes Rocky an odò kāshmīrī dam gōsht

pepper steak   hea : *where?*

mua: in front of heroes & foes

konei: *here* she wishes Rocky moe: *sleep*

passage in not an abebuu adekai fashioned like his teppanyaki

but his speedboat severing Bullwinkle's spleen

somewhere in Iceland she wishes Rocky jouk & Wonderbras abundant

two centerfolds for the price of one   a rave in his name

a place where he eats his celestial tsujiura senbei

uru : *enter* again the binghi harps played by Duke Lukela

he's finally escaped the Blacks and the Jews

Unagi
(an acquired taste)

It is said that eels can come back to life. Chopped into tidbits, left alone, the pieces may regenerate, wiggle: grow new heads, eyes. Teeth. The girl thinks of this every time she eats sushi. She never eats eel two days old. What if it came back to life and paid her a visit one shifty night?

She met an eel one Sunday while playing with pencils and shoestrings. Enthralled by her youth, he invited her into his dollhouse suite for sweets and conversation. The suite was paved with peach bathroom tile. Curtains with oranges hung heavy from iron branches. He was curious about her origins.

What do you look like? he said teasing. *I look like Thumbelina in hand-me-downs,* she said. *You look like a buoyant pocket-sized queen surrounded by a porcelain sea,* he said. *I look like Thumbelina lost in a forest of cows drunk on Night Train,* she said. *I wonder what you look like,* he said. *Inside,* he said. *May I see what you look like inside?* Unable to question his metaphor, she nodded yes.

The bright suite was cold and sweaty. Shards of heat could not alter the

temperature nor spoil the fruit. Stiff he failed once. Slack he failed twice. Caught off by a shriek, the eel bitterly withdrew his solicitation. Outside, a cow was awakening. The eel would not see her insides.

The slimy flesh of an eel always puzzles her. Once unappealing, it has now become an acquired taste. Every morsel that enters her is followed with contemplation. She wonders if its amputations resurrect and swarm in her bowels; if an eel's descendants can finally see what she looks like inside.

have you forgotten any personal property?

dummy check   keys dummy dummy check check
dummy check dummy   my song check check dummy dummy
dummy check   ziploc dummy dummy check

dummy check dummy   black check check
dummy check   dummy dummy love check
dummy check   DAX check check check

dummy check   red check dummy check
dummy check   dummy hot comb dummy dummy
dummy check dummy   bliss check check dummy dummy
dummy check   flash drive dummy dummy check

dummy check dummy   tongue check check
dummy check   dummy dummy headphones
dummy check   code switch check dummy politic

dummy check dummy   check blackness dummy
dummy check dummy   voice check phoneme check
dummy check   prayer check dummy check
        dummy check   check origin *what is...*

dummy check   reservoir dummy dummy dummy check
dummy check   self check affect
dummy check   black red red black check

dummy check dummy   worth check check
dummy check   my name check check dummy dummy
dummy check dummy   lavender lollipop dummy dummy check check
dummy check   dummy dumb dumb *dah*...

who you callin' a jynx?

(after mista popo)

What you wearing on yo' head?
What's that shit on your head?

    Good lord, you make my eyeliner sweat pika twins.
    Peep this joint, I ain't feeling your vibe easy breezy.
    No shogun coming from your tongue.

Mista Popo, mista Tom,

    you queasy.

Where's your flying rug, homie?
Yama-uba bored, my agents gonna reward nada.
I shuffleboard smooches in the land of the rising sun's cosplay, papa.

    ROUGELA COMING STRAIGHT ON YOUR STEREO!
    POPO WHY YOU TRIPPIN LIKE I'M NO-GO!
    POPO YOU A HELLA STRANGE YU-GI-OH!

What your ma said about a Zwarte Piet?
I'll Tilburg to Finland all over her miffy.

    You butterfly gardener,
    I'll make ya choke on a Ricola™.

What the fuck did they do to your lips?
What they do to your lips?

Turban-Hammer-slacks-wearing-pansy.

Get back to Aladdin's bottle,
I battle laughable cannibals.
I induce sleep with my mammaries.
Kiss attack, ya feel me?

Kettei. Mista Popo I'm a thriller.
Rosie flappers for lips.
The most obscene fish queen you ever seen.
Don't Superflat matte my color.

I'm your Yokai nigglet sippin' lovely

with black/purple flesh supposedly offensive.
make no difference in variation,
check it: cross pollination.

Watashi wa zasshu = mass circulation.

Kokujin wanna mark me; I got ya kawaii kiddies.

Popo, here's your "black mammy"
multi-platinum crowd-pleaser,

destroyin’ daisy cutters like legend of the Overfiend skeezas.

I’m causin’ adolescent seizures wit my kage gamma rays.

Hirojima’s in my pocket, epileptics I dare you to rock it.

    muteki dianetics? ya can’t *handle* it!

    Hater-aid bitches mocked my February spin;
    my animated fade-in inori smackin’ gaijins.

Sun, where’s your brain damage comin’ from?

    Why kris kringle got a ocean liner north of the equator.
    Cookies and cream soapland souvenir -
    I polish it with my wamono brassiere.

    ya can’t *handle* it!

      I’m the master puppeteer in my kaiju dynasty
      and you wanna ride me in your tugboat?

What you know about my ice flight?
Wiggle till you figure Harajuku thoughts.

Don’t front,   *you know I got you open.*

    I swing my chariots low for a reason.

mungkin(mencintai)mungkin

possibly (to love) maybe

taisetsu na tu mio guagua nyamuk
how beloved you my baby mosquito

engkau imponente gila murasaki buaya
you awesome insane purple crocodile

karakau mi cinta sampai saya chi es habuk
ridicule me love until my blood is dust

taisetsu na tu mio guagua nyamuk
how precious you my baby mosquito

un aislado kelasi mungkin ninaru nyanyuk
a lonely sailor might grow senile

dakedo, espero para kisu, muda bula mata
although, I wait for a kiss, a young eyelash

taisetsu na tu mio guagua nyamuk
how beloved you my baby mosquito

engkau imponente gila murasaki buaya
you awesome insane purple crocodile

no te entiendo

Check my dialect from my diaphragm.
Buckshot of *Black Moon*

My head is a bony guitar, strung with tongues, plucked by fingers and nails.
Bob Kaufman

la loca ningyo

el oishii zutsu creó gran confusíon
The delicious headache caused havoc.

y la ningyo, gunya-gunya y flaueza, fue bebido.
and the mermaid, flabby and weak in character, was drunk.

se comio el subarashii arufabeto a todo la carrera,
She'd rushed through the admirable alphabet,
canto canto, jinruigaku.

singing anthropology.
"no podemos hacer mucho mas con sekiri"
"There's not much we can do with dysentery."

ni se me pasó por la cabeza que tu
It never entered my head that you were
una yochi na zasshu.

a childish mongrel.
en eso donguri gijutsu, no me interesa.
that acorn technique, I'm not interested.

¡isha! ¡bokusa! ¡estupefacto sagishi!
¡Doctor! ¡Boxer! ¡Superficial swindler!
¿hace mucho que esperas?

¿You've been waiting long?
¡tenia los dedos en carne viva!
¡My fingers were raw!

¡tenia los dedos en carne viva!
¡My fingers were raw!
¿hace mucho que esperas mi kaku

¿You've been waiting long my
no tatsu no otoshigo?
imaginary sea horse?

April 18th

Persian Princess, O Indian beauty pageant queen,
                    there's nothing wrong with Hebrew.

    Blame it on Mimi; dyslexia subsist mistily.
    Lingual alliterations, expulsing nonetheless.
    Your birthright a name renamed & claimed by the famed deranged.

    "rapturously to one knee & repeatedly professing,"
    your pops hot for Momma aka Joey Potter.

Sweet Toledo, no relation to Speedo.
 Vanilla Ohio pickpocket picket fence.
   Momma defends:
      her fussbudget incarnate weaned off methadone.

    Narconon waving zealots belly flop with the stars.

Daddy ate Momma's placenta. You know that?

Daddy bought an ultrasound:
    Dr. Thomas Szasz made Daddy do it.

      Momma disappeared for 14 days:
      they were planning for you on the 15th

& your Momma *kinda* loves the press.
     & then Daddy made your Momma shut her mouth,

       for in the silence of silent Scientology monsoons,
       you inspire "oh so quiet…oh so still" solitude.

    Your birth a most silent one.
& that dyslexia got to subsisting again.

Where are you, Suri?

      & what about this fringe on top,
      you mini microbe of a Björk?

Though few joined
the original movement
to liberate your Momma,

held by forces we may never understand,

    your name is still wonderful.

O Suri,

    you walk among the underdogs along the Suribachi.
Suri, your pastoral band of Ethiopians stick fight with Coolies in Trinidad.
   Suri, who surrenders to animated lemurs in dinosaur movies;

you tipsy Bavarian flowing over Salman Rushdie's historical universe.

Suri, you rare breed of colors reading at a bookstore near Punjab.
Suri, planning Pashtun trilogies with regard to sightings of Rhea.
You mimic robust gummy grubs in the Amazon suckling lychee.

Suri, not to be found, but discovered in a rare & precious alpaca dreadlock,
who swallows & spits the gelato of Aphrodite.

Suri, unheard yet available in mahogany;
you run Rozelle tonight at the Carnegie Mellon.

Suri, the homozygous,
you freshen ethnonyms.
You're interested in the ways people formulate propositions.
You'll visit Pittsburgh as part of a mathematics symposium.
You'll attain new heights of excellence.

Your exceptional silky helmet
& wondrous luster;

the finest for making top quality ladies coats.

ah   Suri   *you actually exist*

                              you do exist… truly you do
       truly   you do…

anasema kwa haraka

slide a bone beneath Her head

dead sistren inna rush rush. im slide

im vex corpse on di boat. sistren has a

words before im carry on. a bone

to pick wid di fadda of pickny beneath

di bush dem planted wen im gwaan astray. Her

spirit won't join im til all fuckery clears head.

tried n tru im say fadda's head

full-up. im corpse rattle. Her

eyes bulge. "tru yu dagga mi sista beneath

di same tri wi firs kissed. but di likkle bone

wi call yuh sistah finga, inside felt nica dan a

daak cock. mek mi pum-pum so wet, sweet-awt jus slide."

That Other Escobar Family

The grass is cool and from afar Matilda hears the fidgeting of someone's fingers fusing with a shotgun's barrel. Her left ear flutters. She lets her son take one more mouthful of flora. She nudges him to run. She grunts at him to run faster. There's a ringing in the air.
Madre sagrada salva mi hijo... Pepé protegelo.

She watches him enter the river.

Matilda mourns for her lover Pepé. Strolling beside a great tangle of leaves and boles, where the treetops supply her canopy, she laments his passing. In the land of treasure and trouble, the horror of seeing him groaning is stuck. She can still picture the bullets lodged in his back. Farmers of plantain and yucca say her tears swell the river often. Her eyes can no longer face the sun.
Al menos nuestros jóvenes sobrevivirán, she says to herself. She thinks, often.
Al menos él sobrevivirá a todo esto.

Matilda has hidden away from all the media attention. She's been a master at hiding deep in the river, wading alongside: feeding on the blade grass since carrots and salt were no longer possible supplements. Frequently, government agents have waded into the Magdalena in hopes of catching her and her young. They don't want the son to be an invasive reminder. She doesn't either. That's why the family escaped the lagoon when they did. Hacienda Napoles' Zoo was no place to raise a child.

Su padre era tal toro, she says to herself. And yes, Pepe was a bull. *Para pensar, cuánto hemos viajado desde nuestro lugar de nacimiento.* And yes, they had traveled quite a bit before settling in Colombia. *Un dia,* she bellows to her calf, *nos podrá nadar más lejos que nunca tenemos y verás la tierra de su papá. Le prometo esto.*

At night, the pelican and iguana hear the young hippo's cries echoing against the bush. He's been submerged since the passing of his mother, since a bullet found its way through her left ear. In this land of extremes, the locals who collect sand say she visits him often in the form of a hummingbird. If one is still, they can see her guiding him into shallows. Look hard enough, and one may see the bush sway and divide fiercely near the ruins of Medellín.

Wallowing in the Magdalena River, he bellows. There is no herd to welcome him. No one is kind enough to echo back to him. And no one directs him towards his papa's land, far across the water.

border universe

ñoqa chutarayani.
I lie.

        ñoqa kani llulla qhapaq de uno *sueño*
            I am a noble liar   from a dream

y ñoqanchis tiyanchis chinkakunapi hatun ch'aki.
    and we live in a large dry labyrinth.

kunan   por que ñoqa,   la luna,
right now   *because of me,*   *the moon,*

urmanki patanpa.
        falls over the edge.

conmi rakhu avalancha
with   my husky avalanche

          o icha,   mi puntiagudo personalmente.
          or perhaps,   *my sharp pointed personality.*

yawrani ch'iñi layqakuna a uspha.
i burn   tiny   witches   to ash.

qankuna sutiyankichis t'ikakunay   neon wayronqopakuna
you all nickname   my flowers   neon botflies

        por que
        because

k'anchanku   una tuta sumaq.
they illuminate   a gorgeous night.

qankuna chhapchikichis,
you all shake,

                chhachukuna machu phiña.
                dressed like old wrathful beggars.

ñoqa yapani sisikuna upa wirasapa, en manka puka   lloqlla.
I add silly fat ants   into a pot,   break all bounds.

        qhepa a horno   t'anta thaka kachi.
        subsequent to baking   dense salt bread.

icha ñoqanchis kankanchis sisikunay, t'akarinchis q'atapa verdad
perhaps we will roast my ants,   spill the muddy truth

en qasi wasiy.
in my vacant home.

        qan khuyapayanki para urpikuna.
        you feel sorry   for   doves.

icha, ñoqa urmani patanpa   o   chhuchuni   en una thaka orgía.

perhaps, I will fall over the edge or slide   silently   into a dense   orgy.

icha, un   remedio ñawpa

perhaps,   an ancient   remedy.

My First Black Nature Poem™

there is a dark mass following me. these legs are clumsy. they flap quickly.
I want to slow them down. but my nerves. *Lord*, these pensive endings.

the sun slumps against the merging fall on red leaves.
and *where the natives are unenlightened,* the mass comes closer.

     only white people swim in lakes nowadays
     you know…Crystal Lake?

never seen a black person jump in a lake;
let alone a river till this summer.
the Bronx River is said to be clean: we care about clean.
a month before, two boys drowned in the Bronx River.
a week after, a boy jumps into it unfazed.

abandoned tires, relics of its sewer days, river herring spark no fear.
and a publicly funded park with a biology class, a boat-making workshop
for the children of Hunt's Point, gives me hope we'd wet our hair again.

  (these follicles don't surf; don't swim)

but here in Virginia, there's little comfort.
the blush current from underwater springs makes me tense.

white people form groups to paddle on boards across the Hudson,
taking on trends from Hawai'i. they tap into the yesterdays
of Algonquian tongues. Wappinger. Mohican.

a sporty new aged (like gouda) convenience.
a luxury to admire when Long Beach is too far
and Rockaway too dirty.

black folk don't swim. we splash and cool off.
we a ways forward from a Splenda hint of Senegalese manliness diving from a ferry,
miles off shore from Gorée. that water got too much memory.
we much prefer chlorine. that salt and fresh water our hypertension.

and that ocean is curiously scary.
and this lake is charmed and churning with tales from the deep.

profound is this river of B-rated torture.
deep are shadow people speculated through my rave tangerine goggles.

on Lake Champlain at night, the chilly air felt like a presence.
swamp monsters (this ain't a swamp). tubular amphibians (they'd be in rivers).
aquatic reptilians. ancestors distraught and vengeful (like Jason).

but this is smaller and gnawing like chiggers; something from my weed days
could live. down. here.

my arms fight the green clearness. so mud olive I cannot see the bottom.
beneath me is crisp. a fallen branch is mistaken for an eel.

trail mix

tilth is a womb. craven is the banana lost at sea. it
needs jesus like all heathens do. wasted corn kernels, the shame! is
what spilt not life? into the spume semen dies. all
alive wading. all normal. dead. abnormal. wading. about
40 million each jack. stumpy dates, copious eggplants lacking the
guidance of anal governments. American sperm needs our love!
there's a crisis and the *strapping Norse* is winning. and
thahn long seed is more exotic than Bronzeville peanuts making
double penetration pop on ghetto-tube. globules of little tails sure
to be tarnished. fertile lubes: Viagra, turkey baster fatalities. we
cherish our melon busboys and mulberry janitors. look
towards Brazil for a sign: passion fruits shaped like man's sex. out-
law the neglect of apples. outlaw the abuse of pumpkins. against, not for
the test tubes. *god gets quite irate* over dried up grapes. men's
spurned daggers bound for banks. drunk fruit flies crave, bemoan sexual
healing from hand. or mouth. seamen think little of the nation's health.

¡cucumber!

Te llama la pīkake loli. Tu eres onaona ni nalu.
>*Your name is jasmine cucumber. You are fragrant like waves.*

Cuando un azotador dàgbà en una luminous àjànàkú,
>*When the caterpillar grows on a luminous elephant,*

¡ano kāna'ohe ese láísí sus sirena de Pu'ukapu!
>*¡the fisherman is without his siren from sacred hill!*

Lucid to 'awapuhi que òsò bautizaba ngahuru,
>*Lucid and ginger-like lagoons baptizing autumn,*

Que tanja iglú flirtatious — corría,
>*like tangerine igloos flirtatious — flowing,*

te llama pīkake loli. Tu eres onaona ni nalu.
>*your name is jasmine cucumber. You are fragrant like waves.*

Anata, täo sangre fría: todo ānuenue, nunca un mesuinu.
>*You, so cool: always a rainbow, never a bitch.*

"Le encantar flitear", "yo se", cantabais Kanaloa.
>*"He's a terrible flirt." "I know," says the god of ocean and wind.*

¿Quien? ¡kána'ohe que ese láísí sus sirena de Pu'ukapu!
>*¿Who? "¡The fisherman that is without his siren from sacred hill!"*

Káne, ele virá tan como trunenos, un ojúlowó in'yu.

> Man, he will come as thunder, a bona fide metaphor.

¿Cuando sus tráfico akemasu, näo vai oerder isto, tá?

> ¿When his traffic opens, you won't lose it, will you?

Te llama pīkake loli. tu eres onaona ni nalu.

> Your name is jasmine cucumber. You are fragrant like waves.

Tan wakarinikui, rebuscaba tua maravilhoso lei pūpū...

> So puzzling, carefully searching your wonderful shell...

Tan tierno, que el mano to puhi to nai'a yurusita.

> So tender, that the shark and eel and dolphin forgave.

¡Tu, kána'ohe ese lâisí sus sirena de Pu'ukapu!

> ¡You, the fisherman that is without his siren from sacred hill!

Todo kemushi amaba kakimono en 'uala y lü'au.

> All furry caterpillars love anything written on sweet potato and kalo leaves.

Me ke aloha pau'ole, una quebra cabeca en köanga.

> So with never-ending love, a jigsaw for your spring.

Te llama pīkake loli. tu eres onaona ni nalu.

> Your name is jasmine cucumber. You are fragrant like waves.

¡Y yo soy kána'ohe ese lâisí sus sirena de Pu'ukapu!

> ¡And I am the fisherman that is without his siren from sacred hill!

marmota monax mizrahi feeds chi chi mugler at the latex ball

call the child legendary:
        tens across for broad plump agrarian fierceness.

marmota monax mizrahi served fur realness for decades.
(it was never about how she bought it. she was born with it.)

no one thought she could battle the twisters —
thought she had retired to a burrow somewhere —
but her arabesque: they gagged & lived for.

her dip-controlled gracefulness said it: shablam! that's how you eat it.

    I am in charge of the gurls,
    don't mind the stubby tray. it's not for you.

the daughters thought they'd turn out the sciurid.
w/ youth & long angular limbs,
    linear rigid action given to geometrics & dramatics;
        something young knees could withstand   but *dis* bitch,

    the undeniable ovahness of marmota monax mizrahi's duck walk sealed it.

    her exhibition. punishing.
    her attack position: cougar cunt realness.
    reinvention: lowland vegan butch.
    the children were not ready.

twisters ate. marmota monax mizrahi broke it down.
spun whirlwinds around cunts bypassing inflamed endorsements.

those short limbs with symmetry sang *"lemme get my life back"*
packaged in Timberland, white tube socks, black latex hot pants.

marmota monax mizrahi tutted her wrists. she refused to be chopped.
spins. catwalk. duck walk. Dips. Dips.
duck walks. lollies. spins. the marmota could not be denied.

"wurk. wurk you woodchuck bitch!" the crowd screamed.

> 13 crowns of tens,
> the trophy placed in her claws
> w/ her final bow,
>
> *"I love you all for loving me."*

krill lassi

A squid eating dough in a polyethylene bag is fast and bulbous. . .got me?
Ed Ruscha

curdle (&) dip. batido it like a .jpg. you thicken like chunky. I am w/o a bubble.

Dear Techserve,

Apparently all has gone to the magic garden. My halophiles were singed when I accidentally used the wrong AC adapter. Could my Sea Monkeys ever be retrieved again? Does my warranty cover this?

It looks like you're writing a letter.
Would you like help?

as serious as a hiccup.

from LimeWire, I download my wonder years. you cite my Prego.
my echo sounder.
my Sazón.

I should have been a pop star. you said this. I know. I should have.
I would have had a bubble by now then...

Dear subscriber,

Despite failed attempts to collect unpaid balances, we have no other choice but to cancel your subscription to the Jacques Cousteau Quarterly.

Please find enclosed a SASE to return the Sea Monkeys and echo sounder. If we do not receive a payment within thirty (30) days, we, mousquemers, will have no choice but to report you to our collection agency.

leeks (&) potatoes. miso (&) tofu. mac (&) velveeta.

I thought we were a biotope together.

metromultilingopollonegrocucarachas
blahblahblah

the train   is castrated by humdrum

joom badaaaaahhhhhh
                             is the aroma of piss and junkies

hoarse covers of lean on me
                stand by me   lean on me

there's a reflection of water bugs' wings
off Snapple bottles rolling back   &   forth

Seeing Eye dogs take up small people space
            rush hour magicians intrude

& while flinging doves
shit on laptop cases

                across the car   peek-a-boo
                buttocks   frazzle orthodox ringlets

                Welcome to Williamsburg

Honduran girls lap dance for Russian divorcés
riding the 6 to 79th to Voice-listed brothels

on the 2   Jamaican Seventh-Day Adventists
          on the seventh
          return to Utica hugging Bibles
          sleeping children

en banda, tomar el numero
uno y nueve uptown

          chicos argentinos   hermosos bronceados
          y pelo largo otro sabor
          sueno con ojos abiertos
          solos de Ceatano Veloso

acostada buttnaked
con Marcos el hermoso

tickkadeeeee   tickkadeetickkadee
tic-tac es pollo pollo y todo   sabe pollo
Marcy Street connects Ecuador to Domsey's Thrift
          middle   earth   relocates
                    Pratt students   to   Do-or-Die
          all   from Iowa

& while the messengers come in Sears sweaters
counting   between   East Broadway & Claremont Ave.
          the train whistles   Yiddish over Korean

          in Gucci boots, falafel calves suffocate
          the   D line

Shabadoo l-boogie
Kims   & Shaniquanas
suck teeth
Old Navy dressing room style

JAPs   eye monkeys exiting Frederick Douglass Blvd.
into Marque 125

where the second-generation twang entices a traffic Cinderella
where roaches pronounce jewelry
as *jury*   liked as *like-ed*

over the   rickkatee tic-tac ticking
ashy Senegalese feet in gold slippers tap tap

so much for underground disturbance

Nihongo in Prada
cross   town to Vanderbilt for feudal bukkake

tickkadee tickkkadee tick tick tick
tic-tac es pollo pollo y el tren es pollo pollo y todo todo sabe pollo

diversion is YOOOOOlanda Vega
on everyone's mind as the monorail enters

World Trade Center
the metropolis subverted
of all subverting time

the broker's watch goes
tickkadeeeeeeeticktock
everyone follows that duration
       ill-dependent on eastern standard
       no one's ever on mountain
       just the path station

& while a Pentecostal woman in overtly modernized
             African attire
       fails to notice the water bug running across her ankle boots

la cucaracha es universal
                y todo todo sabe a pollo

March of the Stylized Natives

the lost verses of kantan pescado

H(@)T DG.I

ti gumadi yu' put ti'ao   I'm not fishing for small fish

baba I mata-mu halu'u   open your eyes baby shark
penta kulot pi'ot labios-mu   color your lips sour plum
hayi malago-mu kilu'os tasi-mu   who do u want my starfish?
oru? kakaguates? faya?   gold? peanuts? anchovies?

51

WP DGJ 🐟🐟

na gumadi yu' put hagu   *I'm casting my net for you*

tife' me. for fresas are jealous   *pick   strawberries*
I fa'gasi my heart of complaints   *wash*
bilembines, one bite I acquaint   *star apple*
taste abas, what kandi! kuanto?   *guava   candy!   how much?!*

YsT DGJ 🐟

when I whistle three times   an' chumefla yu' tres biahi

what would you like to drink?   say this love "hafa gimen-mu?"
             pacific almond   I will say milk of talisai
        what do you want?   then ask "hafa malago'-mu?"
          stand over here   I say tohe guini, surprise me

ᎳᎭᏂᎷ ᎠᏣᎫ 🐟

yute' gadi ya'un falagu.   throw your net and run.

    chunge'-ku, hokka my seedlings   sweet fair stern   pick
from the earth, my eyes too
pa, tupu malago'-hu   pa, sugarcane is what I want
adahi hao, my nest is weak   be careful

HₒT DGↃ 🐟

what pain my mother must have had   gaigi i pinitin nana,

five mosquitoes bit   when lalima namu akka'
her cheeks purple   turning fasu'na lila
octopus afraid   ink like gamson ma'a'nao
          octopus taste good   forgive me, mannge' i gamson

WՐ DGЈ 🐟 🐟

anai para hu ma faniago;   when I was to be born;

chaddeki i apacha   the grasshopper was fast
    kadada' i gua'ot kama   the bunk bed ladder was short
manso i ma'ho ababang   the thirsty butterfly was tame
  machalek estague' mendioka hula   this tapioca tongue was wild

jones

Penitenziagite! Watch out for the draco who cometh in futurum to gnaw your anima! Death is super nos! Pray the Santo Pater come to liberar nos a malo and all our sin! Ha ha, you like this negromanzia de Domini Nostri Jesu Christi! Et anco jois m'es dols e plazer m'es dolors... Cave el diabolo! Semper lying in wait for me in some angulum to snap at my heels. But Salvatore is not stupidus!

Brother Salvatore of Montferrat

from *The Name of The Rose*, Umberto Eco

damn right   it's betta than yours

she getting taught — him getting schooled
    — frosty dips — foamy zouk
         drown dem clods in *kikongo* dollop
        bradda tell a rida — holla at yuh fadda
           — yu in yuh caddy —
             ricochet feed yu — barrington

      di seagulls crack clam shells —
        sailors — da kine stuffin' swelled snails

dey navy yard smiles chinky — cause dey drown dem clods in *kikongo* dollop

    shantay yuh stay — dem — *yard fowl* — serve
swim in *kaiso* — hotel drive — milk dem *lick mouth* — holiday den
assified — technique drop — kikongo dollop — blocka-blocka
    erode di pentameter — blocka-blocka
      shadows sashay — freak-a-leek
        milk dem — hotel drive — bum by — don a dime
        — true dat fadda — charge dem clods
      shantay yuh thesis — walk tick *short tongue*
    — squint when ya milk shake —
        drown dem clods — charge dem clods
          seagulls on crack — blocka-blocka

black herman's last asrah levitation
at magic city, Atlanta 2010

This exclusive shit I don't share with the world.

50 Cent

I, Herman, made medicinal — concocted potions in ways my former's was hearsay;
Turned palomas christened Zora on to formulas husbands roll over n mitzvah.

I, a black lad, proud Virginian, selling out Liberty Hall n pinched w/ stickpins
in Woodlawn, do bequeath my next-to-last oratory:

> My roots subverted the man,
> honeys n dog voyagers to Neptune,
> who dared interfere w/ your melodious saccharine midsection.
> My cluster of tricks made chaps seek out connotation.

> Look at my magic stick.
> Not my clavicles, but my magic stick.

> Ain't no lightness of hand but of bounce player.
> Constraints imposed by a corvid named Jim
> could not interpret my remedies.

> *Jim wasn't much of a MacGyver:*
> *not one skill in therapeutic thaumaturgy.*
> *He prescribed cowlicks for the heartsick: I mean, really.*

But let me tell you something:

Since I am that laconic brother who knows
how to zone in matter untouched n unseen.
When a honey wails "St. James Infirmary"
for my bones that were laid on the fiftieth funeral,

　　　my suspended distortion shall know when to arise n eviscerate.

Now you see me. Now you don't.
Sign up for the joy cruise Shorty.
Mars is the Republic of New Afrika.

　　　　I am the Cyrano of Calvin Cadorzar's drawl.
　　　　A straight-laced shoe herbalist;
　　　　colon cleaner than a chlorophyllian Dappa Don.
　　　　Wanna ride coach to Blue Flame w/ me?

In 1918, I told Quanah Parker, "Jack, Jesus is Peyote!
Said so in the cards — say it ain't so?"

T-Bone hit it straight for 2.50 (even caught a little change on the box),
cause the planets were so aligned.
Sho'nuf heard these arcane words precise.

I am the other.

　　　　Now ain't you a pretty saltshaker.

Sing Sing couldn't hold me down:
I compliment n shatter upstate.
The roots I baked allowed communion w/ God n the dead

In Kentucky I formulated polar bear toe gazpacho —
an elixir for ATLiens — no need to name drop;

just informing you of the origins.

                              Comes in Georgia Peach flavor.
                              Too much will turn your guts like
                              Entheogen.

I patented 'Poo Tang' every morning for AC Powell's breakfast:

            18-ounce glass, ½ Tang & ½ Vodka.

It's good for clairvoyance.
That one on the house.

Dare to transpose any other energy drink, sookie?
This exhumation bears no map
fore the next internment there shall be no other.

            I AM on some other shit.

How delightful you could *clap* to the procession.

I come with black cat bones, Van Van oil n goofer dust.

Lucky numbers. Banjo. Torches. Shells. Dice. Florida water. Do-re-me bush.
Bush meat. Rhino balls. Palo Santo. Duppy Basil. *Hoodoo* muthafucka.

Always to arise on the fourth day: every seven years.

No. You see me.

daggering kanji

k'k'kumu   kk'kk'khakis   k'k'kare   kk'kk'amikazae

k'k'ku'ulala *k'k'ku'ulala*   *k'k'ku'ulala*   *k'k'ku'ulala*

k'k'kazoo   kk'kk'kūlolo   k'k'kahuna   kk'k'kabob

k'k'ku'ulala *k'k'ku'ulala*   *k'k'ku'ulala*   *k'k'ku'ulala*

k'k'kali   kk'k'kulisap   k'k'kabuki   k'k'kk'kumala

k'k'ku'ulala *k'k'ku'ulala*   *k'k'ku'ulala*   *k'k'ku'ulala*

k'k'krill   k'k'kk'kosher   k'k'kolohe   k'k'kk'kinkajou

k'k'ku'ulala *k'k'ku'ulala*   *k'k'ku'ulala*   *k'k'ku'ulala*

k'k'kunan   k'k'kk'kinky   k'kk'karma   k'k'kosdu

k'k'ku'ulala *k'k'ku'ulala*   *k'k'ku'ulala*   *k'k'ku'ulala*

k'k'kola   k'k'k'kitíkití   k'k'kanapī   k'k'kk'king

k'k'ku'ulala *k'k'ku'ulala*   *k'k'ku'ulala*   *k'k'ku'ulala* k'k'kudos   k'k'k'kanatsi   k'k'klutzy   k'k'k'kawoni

k'k'ku'ulala   *k'k'ku'ulala*   *k'k'ku'ulala*   *k'k'ku'ulala*

k'k'kawí   k'k'kk'kawaya   k'k'kao   k'k'k'kamama

k'k'ku'ulala   *k'k'ku'ulala*   *k'k'ku'ulala*   *k'k'ku'ulala*

k'k'koga   kk'kk'kung-fu   k'k'kimchi   k'k'k'kiru

k'k'ku'ulala   *k'k'ku'ulala*   *k'k'ku'ulala*   *k'k'ku'ulala*

k'k'kaliwohi   kk'kk'kumquat   k'k'kina   kk'k'kanogeni

k'k'ku'ulala   *k'k'ku'ulala*   *k'k'ku'ulala*   *k'k'ku'ulala*

k'k'kinetic   kk'k'kanoheda   k'k'kapu   cc'cc'cum

the originator

here's the remedy for your chronic whiplash —

    coming to you via triple ones on a mission —

        pop a wheelie for originators of the flash.

            check ya dial, emboss the rock b4 a fella dip dash.

                grand to slam a party — peep two needles in collision:

        here's the remedy for your chronic whiplash.

      flare your dome w/ a pinch of cheeba succotash—

    got my avenue peaking rapid circumcision —

pop a wheelie for originators of the flash.

    ululate the call; gods never caught tongue-lash —

      tweak an EQ. my hash sparks double vision:

        here's the remedy for your chronic whiplash.

            got my tambourine for ya partner. pass the calabash.

        smile for the DJ when the cut spits — peep the precision.

      pop a wheelie for originators of the flash —

never fret what the beat can establish in the trash.

master meter on Orion, starship blast w/ supervision:

    here's the remedy for your chronic whiplash —

      pop a wheelie for originators of the flash.

gamab click
the bedouin remix

                                        light up di egret's plumage
                    dey sky needles di record on dey turntable of epiphany proudfoot
blazin' pele's bass line over runneth di clouds wit kravitz's arrows

        in di rain di blanc-mange seeps from dey dirt
                in di mountains maestro spare a seed n sow in peyote stitch

ink loves dey ache; loves dey gamab magma
    so *listen sparrow hawk that holds the keys to the orient*

                                    cut n burrow yo' former maverick
                            waist beads don't conjure ambrosia
                    down by di lakeshore we pray fo oxala's rain

        garuda is a buzz kill   der goes alfalfa wit a dark n lovely
        der behest his *unabomber's* sound clash straddlin' vishnu's skillet

        a chicken   a waffle   a blizza of day lilies
streams of bittersweet synth blarney

                        swing low my nephrite pendulum
                    shake a birdlime from di crow's tales
            we see yo' hair bucklin' dem bongo naps

we got a mouth of yo' pink tutus undulatin' funky worms

wee wee   strum madame   blackamoors
we were   *a*   *very*   *good nigger*

there still remains one sea to cross

wee wee   strum madame   blackamoors
we accept   we *accept it all*

a moonful a spoonful a suga tit
let dey high hat make water from yo' hang glider
dis name jigga boo velveteen fraggle rock agogo funk

di wind spit at your ravens
make nickels tickle mandingo saviors

no appropriatin' of tongues jigga jigga   HOO   true   you knew ja rule

Curl

wi taught in Home Ec. holim our ti that

rot. dat pinky (etiquette fo da poor), an organdy

digit bent or improperly straight fo jokes. pillow

memory namba tu. slender organic coke spūn to

sample: dat dragon tip bikmama used to never

salim us spotted wit crusty yau. she curl

her pinga into canals; scoop & clear. irony against

every *suga straw*. teacha gift: porcelain ti set fo me.

gamin'gabby

Syraniqua D'Voidoffunk...

trust your fields of prayers won't summon this earth,

       where mountains crash beneath an ocean's thrust.
lonely words burn still days; you mime breech birth.

you flee before the dawn makes jest to trust.

       what good are rainbows, whispering surprise,
or waterfalls that dine with a tongue's dreams?

this smile falls mute: all's left are toys and lies.

       this joy flies while showers return dazed screams;
rude boyish nature truth dares hide n seek.

your tag balls merry go's or building bricks,

       this morning, leave my pulse free of fool's tricks.
a rabbit's speed, a thousand miles by week.

       these eyes awake and hear the sun;

       good are flints when the night's cherub has spun.

Cyré Komaki...

chulo, whining is not for the strong at heart.

                you have a vice to sweat the ills when no one is sick.

      where are the stars when you sleep all day? what

    good are southern memories that keep you sprung? no
      one said the text message was an exercise,
            so why respond like you vibin' at length, bitch?

          don't you know it's ten cents a message, playa?

     don't tease my eyes when you fall short.

          I'll blame my ovaries before I consider again.

     my feathers ruffled from yo' dusty mane,
    the moon, the tides, the ripples, the love below!

        I'll give dawn to vanity, smoke you, tag you wack.

your bluff, don't bother to ring, departure time, the 11th hour.

      stay yo' ass up in Gilroy! the sun mighty nice over yonder.

Cyrona Moonwalker...

           baby boy   whin'n ain't   workin'

     you   vizzle ta sweat   baseheads.   no one itchin'

     tha stars?   you sleep all day.   wizzle

         memories,   pussy whipped son.

      text message: thou   art   has   gamed   me.

   yo' aim   off.   beeyotch,   ten cents

a messagizzles?   say it ain't so!   don't teaze

    mah eyes   F-to-tha-izzall   shortie,   test   mah ovaries.

      feathas ruffled;   flakeolicious   head.

tha moon,   tides   ripple   mah   snatch.

    gizzy dawn   ta vanity.   scoot yo' pizzay.

      live n die in Fruitvale,   sun poppin' funkedelic. yonder

     eyes   awakes n hizzy tha sun.

Syralestine Saint-Savin...

ulochay, iningwhay isway otnay orfay ethay ongstray atway earthay

erewhay ountainsmay ashcray eneathbay anway oceansway'say ustthray

erewhay areway ethay arsstay enwhay ouyay eepslay allway ayday,

ouyay eeflay eforebay ethay awnday akesmay estjay otay usttray.

oneway aidsay ethay exttay essagemay asway anway exerciseway,

osay ywhay espondray ikelay ouyay'eray ibinvay' atway engthlay itchbay?

onday'tay ouyay owknay itway'say entay entscay away essagemay?

atwhay oodgay areway ainbowsray, isperingwhay urprisesay,

rway aterfallsway atthay ineday ithway away onguetay'say eamsdray?

iway'llay ameblay ymay ovariesway eforebay Iway'day onsidercay againway.

ymay eathersfay uffledray omfray oyay' ustyday anemay,

ethay oonmay, ethay idestay, ethay ipplesray, inway ymay atchsnay. iway'llay

ivegay awnday otay anityvay, okesmay ouyay, agtay ouyay ackway.

oodgay areway intsflay enwhay ethay ightnay'say erubchay ashay unspay.

mug shot pedigree

tall   brown   mid-frame   bald
tree   bag   suspect residence   average
buzzed   mayhem   clean-shaven
high tower   perpetrator   wood   proportionate
                groomed   tight   crime location

long   pretty
elegant   dark brindle   loose temperament   scalped

6'2"

Breeder(s): unknown at this moment

1 liter   white oak   in custody for   built
                                waves

thirst quencher black strap   thick   boy
40 ounce   muthafucka   kunta kinte   runt of litter
sip of _____   peculiarities   mighty joe young
jet   case number: 1349, 2012-103-6306
                                                overgrown

        extremely dangerous

        deep plum   baby Daddy   DMX
                waxed   certified   stud
        broad   champion   du rag

smooth   laid back   shoulder
front   & rear   strong & balanced

Sylvester Corey Roberts, A661126, Black Male
Whelped: 05-07-85, Stud Book: 12-87; A.K.A Phieggy Boo

Tests: [OFA Good 03-17-87, SLT/PRA 05-87, Clear, CS 2644G33F]
F.B.I. #360755CB1
[SIRE: Pierre Roberts(?) Daryl Eugene Dryer (?) Roderick Otis Tanner (?)]
[DAM: Juanita Mackie Roberts]

(Boo Yaa)

'ā'ī neck   protect ya deck.
kīkala hip skip like yo booty don't care,
cause you can't maintain the funk,
I'm the doo-wop millionaire.
      the doo-wop-wop debonair,   sipping wai belvedere.

      my ihu nose lines the prize
      sipping hua'ai belvedere
              belvedere
           belvedere
              sipping wai hua'ai belvedere

I'm so clean. check. fresh. check. fly. so def.
yes yes y'all,   Pele comes to wreck.

      knee deep as I speak,   kino body rock.
lehelehe wit the glock
of menehune.   freak of the week   you's a pua'a at a lū'au.

      my hand lima blazes like Ka'ahupahua.
      maka *dope-a-delic* like Redman in a hula.

let me tell it:
I'm taking cheek papālina,
poli breast feedin' malihini dust schemas.

wit da force of my Momma's
devil's walking stick.
po'o   head trip!
oh you's a dumb haole chick.

your mush waha just pixie dust in my shells,

pu'uwai like my nose,
take it right back to the cell…

my ihu nose lines the prize, dressed to the nines.

I'm so clean. check. fresh. yes. fly. so def.
yes yes y'all,   Pele comes to wreck.

King Sani, the mystical crotch
while listening to The Mars Volta's "This Apparatus Must Be Unearthed"

to panther to a small house cat.
      to sand to dust to water to metal.
            the flesh chalk. the crotch. top secret

      phallus fantasia & relaxed pain,
is said to walk through bedlam walls.

to Gary to monkeyshine to Brazil to water to combustion.

            the prodigal bulge overwhelms.
        it is a bubblegum kink.   a Sheikh's interloper.
    a radical since 1979. a brujo. a tommy gun. a werewolf.
    a Kudos-derived crotch screaming at his maharashi;
        this crotch is a rollercoaster —
           it radiates beside Pavarotti.

it makes uncouth melody mill about in Nederland.
it is a holistic crotch with dynamic roundabouts.

 a sleight of the hand,
  a nip a tug a tuck,
    the bulb achieves menagerie.

to Peter to pinga to muscle fingering gestures,
the crotch has had a speculative center.
even in black & magnetic red rags,
its tantrum is a Ferris wheel.

this crotch has radar, fancies the shattering of glass bottles,
serenades to black supermodels & playboy Jheri curls.

it plods the gravel,
pleads to molt & spill.

it is a riveted masquerader. military jacket adorner.
this machinery long patented since boyhood chitterling boners.

a conveniently omitted crotch,
so weighed down the bulge was never appraised.
(just burrowed into a world parable.)

never fashioned into a plaything priced at $12
its head is engorged,
& polished scrotum taut.
its bad boy innuendos became encrusted
with conflict-free Swarovski.

no one heard the howls
from its flaccid state leveling the skies,
so it awoke the dead,
& demanded petitions.

were the gods that crazed to create such a sensationalized crotch?
did the universe ever welcome this quiver shifter?

pry, the giving crotch pries.
this is a charitable crotch.
root, the naïve rotting crotch makes roots.
this was a charitable crotch.

to skin flesh. to make skeletons throb.
   to make royalties roll n dribble during nocturnal emission.
      to Moonwalker to Fred Astaire to James to a yard made from
         two nervous bodies.
               to become a pelvic jolt clad in leather & metallic cod straps.

                  thud & thrusts calculate
         a jackhammer. a bolt fixed in the camera lens.
                  the crotch wanted to be a deity,
         but later auctioned off tatty penny loafers.

         it collapsed & minces the dirt now;
         it is a crotch that once directed winds,
               resurrected elephants,
                  freed dolphins.

to
   become Dracula. to
      become crooner. to
      become a wall.
            the crotch no longer desires to spin gold thread,
               something it now admits is foolish to replicate.

oceania

Afta dat, dey talk up. Dey not so scared fo speak up anymo.
Lisa Linn Kanae, *Sista Tongue*

symphony para ko'ko i gamson

(symphony for a octopus harvest)

bo'ok i constraints para como comprenda.   *pull out the constraints for who understands.*

hale' i ensemble.   *dig up the ensemble.*

estague *close.* to the throat.

    maila' halom paluma yan trumpets.   *come in birds and trumpets.*

kao nuebu i fruition?   *is the fruition hot?*

maila' guini. enaogue' aparté de hula'-hu virgin,

    come here. away from your **dalaga** *tongue,*

i talanga-na un kakaibá volante.   *his ear is a queer ruffle.*

    na'chocho i symbiosis   *feed the symbiosis*
    tohge guini eyague'.   to his ear.

tanom i capacities sa'   *plant the capacities because*

i talanga-na un kakaibá volante.   *his ear is a queer ruffle.*

bula i gimen-hu kapatíd na lalaki. *your drink is full brother.*

baba i kuatto-mu. *ga'ga'* burst. *stand here. close. **sumambulat** open your room animal.*

pasto i firefly siha. *put the **alitaptáp** to pasture.*

baba i petta para si kuminóy. *open the door for quicksand.*

hunggan, attilong i cluster manglo' cactus.

*yes, the cluster is a black wind **hagdambató**.*

"I know not how the truth may be,
I tell the tale as 'twas told to me."

A **DⱦꝞꝬꝼ** ^{agehya} had become too concerned with what others were thinking about and forgot her daughter was sitting beside the river. By the time she remembered, the child was missing. She began to search the bank and found nothing and began to cry. A raven flew by and saw the woman crying and asked what upset her so. She told the raven that she had lost her daughter and asked if the raven had seen her. The raven shook his head and told her that he had seen **JꝹY** *Gûle'gĭ*, the great climber, eating by the river. The woman hurried up the bank where she found **JꝹY** *Gûle'gĭ*, the great black snake, finishing his feast. "**JꝹY** *Gûle'gĭ*, have you ate my daughter? I can't find her," she asked. **JꝹY** *Gûle'gĭ* lifted his head and said, "No, I did not, but if you are looking, maybe you should ask **ꞒꝦꝦ** *Wa'huhu'*, Screeching Owl." Then **JꝹY** *Gûle'gĭ* slithered off and left the woman. The woman went into the forest in search of **ꞒꝦꝦ** *Wa'huhu'*, praying that she would find her daughter by chance. She finally came to a large holly tree and found **ꞒꝦꝦ** *Wa'huhu'*, whose eyes were red as hot stones. The Sun was going down and the woman knew it would not be long before the night seers were hunting for food. She reached up and shook a branch until she got **ꞒꝦꝦ** *Wa'huhu's* attention. "**ꞒꝦꝦ** *Wa'huhu'*, have you seen my daughter? I lost her along the banks." **ꞒꝦꝦ** *Wa'huhu'* peered down at her and replied no. The woman now in tears muttered, "**ꞒꝦꝦ** *Wa'huhu'*, please help me. I've lost my daughter and the forest is thick and the night seers will soon be awake and hungry. Can you help me?" **ꞒꝦꝦ** *Wa'huhu'* spread his black scorched feathers and took to the air. As **ꞒꝦꝦ** *Wa'huhu'* flew between the trees, he came across **ꝎJJ** *U'guku'* and **ꝞYꝒ** *Tskĭlĭ'*, Hooting Owl and Horned Owl. "**ꝎJJ** *U'guku'*, there is a woman looking for her daughter. Have you seen her?" **ꝎJJ** *U'guku'* had just awakened and had seen nothing. "**ꝞYꝒ** *Tskĭlĭ'*, have you seen the woman's daughter? She may be mistaken for someone's dinner if she's not found." ᏥᎩᎵ*Tskĭlĭ'* looked at ᏩᎱᎱ*Wa'huhu'* and answered. "I have not seen the child, but I did see ᎧᎾᏁᏍᎩ ᎠᎹᎢᏰᎯ*Kănăne'skĭ Amai'yĕhĭ*, the Water Spider, weaving a very large basket. Perhaps she would know." ᏩᎱᎱ*Wa'huhu'* flew back to the woman and told her what ᏥᎩᎵ*Tskĭlĭ'* had told him. "Come sit on my back and hold on. We go see why ᎧᎾᏁᏍᎩ ᎠᎹᎢᏰᎯ*Kănăne'skĭ Amai'yĕhĭ* is weaving such a large basket." The woman did as she was told and together they flew further into the forest to find ᎧᎾᏁᏍᎩ ᎠᎹᎢᏰᎯ*Kănăne'skĭ Amai'yĕhĭ*. When they found ᎧᎾᏁᏍᎩ ᎠᎹᎢᏰᎯ*Kănăne'skĭ Amai'yĕhĭ*, she was indeed weaving a large basket and one too large to carry on her back. ᏩᎱᎱ*Wa'huhu'* flew down and landed on a bush right beside ᎧᎾᏁᏍᎩ ᎠᎹᎢᏰᎯ*Kănăne'skĭ Amai'yĕhĭ*. "ᎧᎾᏁᏍᎩ ᎠᎹᎢᏰᎯ*Kănăne'skĭ Amai'yĕhĭ*," said ᏩᎱᎱ*Wa'huhu'*, "Why are you making such a large basket?" "I make the basket for a girl I found in the forest. I plan to take her to ᏕᎷᏂᎳᏧ*Nûñdâgûñ'yĭ*, the Sun land in the East, where she will be safe. The forest too dangerous for a small child." ᏩᎱᎱ*Wa'huhu'* told ᎧᎾᏁᏍᎩ ᎠᎹᎢᏰᎯ*Kănăne'skĭ Amai'yĕhĭ* that she could stop because the child's mother was here. "ᎧᎾᏁᏍᎩ ᎠᎹᎢᏰᎯ*Kănăne'skĭ Amai'yĕhĭ*, please tell me where she is," the woman begged. ᎧᎾᏁᏍᎩ ᎠᎹᎢᏰᎯ*Kănăne'skĭ Amai'yĕhĭ* led the woman to a sycamore tree that held the first fire given to them. Beside the tree was her daughter asleep under a blanket woven by ᎧᎾᏁᏍᎩ ᎠᎹᎢᏰᎯ*Kănăne'skĭ Amai'yĕhĭ*. The woman was happy and cried until her tears made a river that ran down the mountain. She whispered in her daughter's ear, "I will never leave you alone again." She thanked ᏩᎱᎱ*Wa'huhu'* and ᎧᎾᏁᏍᎩ ᎠᎹᎢᏰᎯ*Kănăne'skĭ Amai'yĕhĭ* and took her daughter home. The next day, the woman and daughter moved to Harlem where strawberries were abundant year round.

churp

Birds, he says, have about five things to say.

bon dia. a moment to shush with clock radio. a moment to coo
and flounder the last scene. *féràn èmi.* this haunch misses you. this scalp
has felt neglected since. everyone wants love. not many get it.
get out. go somewhere. go on. this haunch remembers everything. this
scalp admits something. *i found a worm.* you found your fill. i literally
found a buláti. on concrete. in the sun. in a puddle of rain. drowning
and frying. *magandáng gabí.* as if you'll be there to say good morning. as
if another worm could be found with you. as if you'll love me. *tú.*
another alarm clock. another dream. another word. a new word. same
meaning. *good morning. quiéreme. nakita akong kòkòrò. bon nochi. fuera.*
like you said, *all the rest is noise.*

rhinestones, acrylic on panel, knives, mirror, packing tape, fur, found medical illustration paper on mylar, rubber tires, wood, metal, plastic, porcelain, paper, latex paint, Lonely Planet phrase books…

anime

mista popo™ *hollas @ jynx*™ *Ganguro* refers to the Japanese subculture where young girls from Shibuya tan their skin very dark and bleach their hair. The term itself means *black face* whereas gangankuro means *exceptionally dark.*

pistology is a macaronic verse; the poem is written in Japanese, Spanish, and English.

bacche kā pōtrā is Hindi/Urdu for *nappy*. A loose golden shovel (a recent poetic form created by Terrance Hayes after Gwendolyn Brooks), the poem contains the line "wave treetops wave burnt particles wave sirens wave gray perfume." from "eleven maroons" by Fred Moten.

Sunspot is a golden shovel. It contains the line "are we without desire mouthed Who are we in the presence" from the poem "Recite Neruda in my thighs in my open mouth constellatory psalms" by Metta Sáma. *Penor* is Welsh for *headpiece* or *muzzle.*

Benihana is written in Maori, Hawaiian, Japanese, Samoan, English, and some Hindi/ Urdu. Rocky is Hiroaki Aoki, the founder of the Benihana restaurant chain. *Omikuji* is Japanese for fortune slip and the type of cookie often associated with Chinese restaurants. The fortune cookie is said to have been first introduced to America by the Japanese in the early 20th century. Che Fong, Duke Lukela, Kono Kalakaua, and Chin Ho Kelley were characters in the original television series *Hawaii Five-0.*

have you forgotten any personal property? is a response to visual artist Gary Simmons'
Erasure series.

who u callin' a jynx? Superflat refers to the postmodern Japanese art movement led
by Takashi Murakami. Soapland is one of several illegal brothels in Japan where
the client is "washed" by a naked woman covered with soap.

mungkin(mencintai)mungkin is written in Japanese, Malay, English, and Spanish.

no te entiendo

la loca ningyo or the "crazy mermaid" is written in Spanish, English, and Japanese.

April 18th The quote "rapturously to one knee & repeatedly professing…" is taken
from the article "How Personal Is Too Personal for a Star Like Tom Cruise?" by
Sharon Waxman as printed in the *New York Times*, 2005. April 15 is the birthday of
Dr. Thomas Szasz, co-founder of the Citizens Commission on Human Rights
(CCHR), which was established by the Church of Scientology. The lyrics quoted
are from "It's Oh So Quiet" by Björk. Pashtun or Suri is an ethnic tribe in Pakistan
and Afghanistan. Rhea or Suri is a flightless bird native to Patagonia in South
America. The alpaca is a domesticated breed of ungulates related to llamas. There
are two types of alpaca that are defined by their coats: the Huacaya has short and
crumply hair while the Suri has silky dreadlocks.

anasema kwa haraka is Swahili for "she speaks in a hurry." It contains a line from the
poem "The Anniad" by Gwendolyn Brooks.

border universe is written in English, Spanish, and Runa Simi (Quechua).

My First Black Nature Poem™ contains a line taken from the First United Church of the Fisher Price® Record Player website.

trail mix is a golden shovel and contains a quote from the Ohio State Senator Nina Turner. The poem also contains a lyric from Monty Python's "Every Sperm is Sacred." The *strapping Norse* refers to the article "A Baby 'Bjorn' Sperm Crisis, Shortage Hits Wannabe Parents," written by Janon Fisher for *The New York Post* in 2007. In the article, Janon writes, "Couples who once hoped to purchase samples from square-jawed, strapping Norsemen living in Lillehammer will have to settle for locksmiths, bartenders and struggling writers from less exotic locales, such as Bensonhurst, Brooklyn, Rego Park, Queens, and Hackensack, N.J." Thahn Long, also called Sweet Dragon, is a Vietnamese fruit.

¡cucumber! is written in Spanish, Hawaiian, Yoruba, English, Japanese, and Portuguese.

marmota monax mizrahi feeds chi chi mugler at the latex ball contains a line from the song "Elements of Vogue" by David Ian Xtravangaza.

metromultilingopollonegrocucarchasgoulashblahblahblah A section of this poem is written in Spanish. It reads: "In gangs, they take the number / one and nine uptown / Argentine boys beautiful, tanned / and long hair…another flavor / I dream with open eyes / Ceatano Veloso solos / Lying butt naked / with Marcos the beautiful."

March of the Stylized Natives:
the lost verses of kantan pescado

This series of songs is constructed from *kantan chamorritas,* an ancient style of improvised debate or "freestyle" indigenous to the Chamorro natives of Mariana Islands and Guam. In this nearly extinct language, "the term *ayotte,* meaning to throw verses, is significant to this form for it was used in satirical and/or loving exchange between clans and during public feasts" (Wikipedia). Each section is preceded by lines taken from original *kantan chamorritas* that were translated during the 1900s by missionaries. Each verse is preceded with a part of the title of the Dr. Seuss book *One Fish, Two Fish, Red Fish, Blue Fish* in Cherokee (Tsaˊlăgĭˊ).

jones

damn right. . .it's better than yours contains several words from Barbadian dialect. Kaiso is a popular music from Trinidad and several other Caribbean islands. Kikongo (Congo) is one of several African nations that were transported to the western hemisphere and one of many where linguistic traces are still prevalent in what Kamau Brathwaite defines as Nation Language.

black herman's last asrah levitation at magic city, Atlanta 2010. Black Herman, born Benjamin Rucker in 1892, was an African-American magician. He died on stage during one of his performances in 1934. The Magic City, located in downtown Atlanta, is an adult club often mentioned in rap lyrics and featured in rap videos.

daggering kanji is written in Hawaiian, Cherokee (Tsaˊlăgĭˊ), English, Tagalog, Quechua, Japanese, and Maori. Kinkajou, also known as a honey bear, is related to the raccoon and is native to Central and South America.

gamab click the bedouin remix "Unabomber" and "Skillet" are the titles of two songs by Backyard Band. "Funky worms" is the title of a song written by the Ohio Players. The lines in italics come from Aimé Césaire's *Notebook of a Return to The Native Land.* Gamab, the god death in the Khoisan religion of the San and Khoi people of South Africa, lives in the sky and directs the fate of mankind. Associated with the clouds, thunder, and water, he shoots arrows at humans from his black heaven. Anyone hit will die and join him in his village. When they arrive, Gamab offers them a drink from a bowl of liquid fat.

Curl is a golden shovel and contains the line "that organdy pillow to never curl against me" from the poem "Recite Neruda in my thighs in my open mouth constellatory psalms" by Metta Sáma. The poem is written in two pidgins: one from Port Morseby, Papua New Guinea (according to Terry D. Barhorst and Sylvia O'Dell-Barhorst) and the other from Hawai'i.

mugshot pedigree OFA refers to Orthopedic Foundation for Animals. PRA refers to Progressive Retinal Atrophy, which is a hereditary disease of the retina found in most purebred adult dogs.

(Boo Yaa) Portions of this poem are written in Hawaiian after a conversation as to whether rap lyrics could be structured on the page and still maintain both literary and rhythmical integrity. The translation of each word is literally beside it (either before or after the word) indicating a body part. Pele is the goddess of the volcano. Wai hua'ai is a traditional drink from Hawai'i. Haole is a term for white people. Contains lyrics from the song "RID is coming" by the rap group Boo-Yaa T.R.I.B.E.

King Sani the mystical crotch Soon after the release of the *Dangerous* album, Michael Jackson traveled to the Ivory Coast in 1992. There, he consented to being crowned King of Sani in a ceremony conducted under a sacred tree in the gold-mining village of Krindjabo, heart of the Agni tribe near the capital, Abidjan. The coronation took place superintended by traditional chief Amon N'Djaolk, who placed a golden crown on the head of the tribe's new monarch and declared Jackson was now King Sani. He reigned over the tribe for 18 years. Following Michael's death, Jesse Jackson was crowned High Prince of the Agni people of Côte d'Ivoire.

oceania

symphony for an octopus harvest is written in Quechua, Tagalog, Chamorro, English, and Spanish.

"I know not how the truth may be, I tell the tale as 'twas told to me." is written in Cherokee (Tsaʹlăgĭ') and English. The title is taken from *Myths of the Cherokee* by James Mooney.

churp contains words in Tagalog, English, Spanish, Yoruba, and Papiamentu. The quote is from an interview with filmmaker Stan Brakhage on filmmaker Hollis Frampton.

recognize

My father Oxalá, my mothers Iemanjá e Oxum. Thank you for all the blessings you have given me, for all the challenges so that I can learn and grow. You hold me in your arms and wash me with your waters. You help me focus. You love me. It is because of your blessings I am here. It is because of your blessings this book is here. Axé

Some of the poems in this book have or will be published in the various publications:

Puerto del Sol, flyway, fishhousepoems.org, Semantikon.com, belladonna chapbook series, Tea Party Magazine, Rattapallax, The Black Scholar, Palabra, nocturnes (re)view, How(2): Women and Eco-Poetics Issue, Jubilat, Fence, Black Renaissance Noir, LA Review, Mandorla: Writings for the Americas, Journal of Pan-African Literature, Spoken Word Revolution Redux, Gathering Ground: Cave Canem Tenth Anniversary Anthology, and *Villanelles.*

To Rachel Levitsky, Cara Benson, Krystal Languell, Emily Skillings, HR Hegnauer, and the Belladonna Collaborative, I cannot thank you enough.

To Douglas Kearney. Your feedback and equally twisted humor helped tremendously. I credit you for the Tolson quote. One of the magical ingredients in this collection is our conjuring of the dozens and the risks involved with defining poetry in a manner we relate to. You even designed the book cover! To the Kearney family, thank you for your love and for sharing Doug's ears and eyes when I needed them.

To Metta Sáma and Randall Horton, who provided ample nit picking and suggestions. To Jamie Helper, Kevin Simmonds, Duriel E. Harris, Rodrigo Toscano, Teresa Walsh, Guillermo E. Brown, Israel Francisco Haros, Monica Hand, Yosara

Trujillo, Brian Teare, Tara Betts, Sharifa Rhodes-Pitts, Greg Tate, Urayoán Noel, Quincy and Margaret Troupe, Krista Franklin, Edwin Torres, Kathleen Fraser, Donna de la Perrière, Petrushka Bazin, Erica Hunt, Rashida Bumbray-Shabazz, Gabri Christa, Marilys Ernst, Vernon Reid, Tonya Foster, Mendi and Keith Obadike, and Tyehimba Jess. All of you provided tutelage, knowledge, friendship, support, and at times, a good meal and movie tickets. If I have somehow failed to mention you, lo siento. Know that I recognize and appreciate you sincerely. To the disbelievers: *shofsekle*.

I must acknowledge the New York Foundation of the Arts, Virginia Center for the Creative Arts, Pocantico, Lower Manhattan Cultural Council, Caldera Arts, the Eben Demarest Trust, the Mayer Foundation, The Jerome Foundation, Harlem Community Arts Fund, The Laundromat Project, and Change Inc, as they provided me a place to work, means to research, funds to pay late rent, bury my mom, purchase a new computer, video cassettes, paper and ink, and made my life as an artist a little easier.

To the Cave Canem family, to Cornelius, Toi, and Sarah, your love for black poetry has taught me the value of creating community and opportunities to advance the poetry of black and brown folk. To Carolyn Micklem, you always believed and for that, this book is in your honor.

To Denise and Elizabeth who would talk shit about me in Spanish when I was 12; to Paula Washington, James Murphy, and Grandfather Bill who taught me Cherokee when I was 16; to the Cherokee Language Circle and Gadugi Community for reminding me over the years; to Suzuki Tomofumi who taught me Japanese in 1996; to Odi Gonzales, who taught me Quechua in 2008; to Hone Bailey who taught me Maori songs in 2009 and to Regina who taught me how to say "cute boys" in Samoan; Wado, Arigato, Kia Ora, Gracias.

To my mommy, Margaret Elizabeth Diggs, and to Akilah Oliver, I miss your smiles and spunk. To Miss Ana Rodriguez, I will miss your encouragement and bright presence in rehearsals. And to Jayne Cortez, I will miss your strength, friendship, mentorship, and our special Thai lunch dates.

Alofa atu oe

Writer, vocalist, and sound artist **LaTasha N. Nevada Diggs** is the author of three chapbooks, which include *Ichi-Ban* and *Ni-Ban* (MOH Press), *Manuel is destroying my bathroom* (Belladonna*), and the album *Television*. Her work has been published in *Rattapallax, Black Renaissance Noir, Nocturnes, Fence, Ploughshares, The Black Scholar,*

Photo by Greg Tate

P.M.S, LA Review, Jubilat, Everything But the Burden, and *Muck Works* among others. Her interdisciplinary work has been featured at The Kitchen, Exit Art, MoMA, Recess Activities Inc, Brooklyn Museum, MoMA PS1, and the Whitney. As a vocalist, she has worked with the likes of Vernon Reid, Akilah Oliver, Mike Ladd, Butch Morris, Gabri Christa, Shelley Hirsch, Jason and Alicia Moran, Burnt Sugar, Edwin Torres, Elliot Sharp, Mendi + Keith Obadike, Bernard Lang, DJ Logic, Vijay Iyer, Ryuichi Sakamoto, Marc Cary, Towa Tei, and Guillermo E. Brown. She has received several scholarships, residencies, and fellowships; among them include Cave Canem, Harvestworks Digital Media Arts Center, New York Foundation for the Arts, the Eben Demarest Trust, Harlem Community Arts Fund, Lower Manhattan Cultural Council, The Laundromat Project, Virginia Center for the Creative Arts, Barbara Deming Memorial Grant for Women, Jerome Foundation Travel and Study Grant, and Black Earth Institute. As an independent curator and artistic director, LaTasha has presented and directed literary/musical/theatrical events at Symphony Space, Lincoln Center Out of Doors, WBAI, The Schomburg Research Center for Black Culture, BAM Café, Dixon Place, and El Museo del Barrio. A native of Harlem, LaTasha and writer Greg Tate are the founders and editors of *yoYO/SO4 Magazine*.

 green
press
INITIATIVE

Belladonna Books is committed to preserving ancient forests and natural resources. We elected to print this title on 30% postconsumer recycled paper, processed chlorine-free. As a result, we have saved:

2 Trees (40' tall and 6-8" diameter)
1 Million BTUs of Total Energy
186 Pounds of Greenhouse Gases
1,010 Gallons of Wastewater
68 Pounds of Solid Waste

Belladonna Books made this paper choice because our printer, Thomson-Shore, Inc., is a member of Green Press Initiative, a nonprofit program dedicated to supporting authors, publishers, and suppliers in their efforts to reduce their use of fiber obtained from endangered forests.

For more information, visit www.greenpressinitiative.org

Environmental impact estimates were made using the Environmental Defense Paper Calculator. For more information visit: www.edf.org/papercalculator